Come Follow *God*

MARIANNA ALBRITTON

Come Follow God
Copyright © 2022 by Marianna Albritton. All rights reserved.

All rights reserved. No part of this book may be reproduced or transmitted in any form or by any means, electronic or mechanical, including photocopying, recording, or by any information storage and retrieval system without express written permission from the author, except in the case of brief quotations embodied in critical reviews and certain other noncommercial uses permitted by copyright law.

Published in the United States of America

Brilliant Books Literary
137 Forest Park Lane Thomasville
North Carolina 27360 USA

DEDICATION

I dedicate this book to my Granddaughter, Abigail Annemarie Albritton. I want to pass on the blessed spiritual legacy handed down by my grandfather, John Quitman, to my mother, Vema, to me, to Matt, to Ben and on to Abigail. May God always be a real and present person to you. Your grandpa and I pray for your knowledge of Jesus and His presence in your life always.

ACKNOWLEDGEMENTS

This is probably the hardest page to write. So many people prayed and encouraged me during this time of writing I am concerned about leaving out someone's name. However, name mentioned or not, I am very thankful for everyone who did pray and speak words of encouragement.

I could not attempt such a task without the editing, suggesting, praying, and sometimes pushing help from Garnet. She has seen me through the hard time period of covid when sometimes I felt absolutely mentally and spiritually paralyzed to accomplish anything. She would not let me give up.

My Sunday School Class, and others encouraged a second book to follow the theme of COME CLIMB TOWARD GOD. Thanks also go to my Pastor Paul Brashier who understands my spiritual gift of teaching and my desire to pass on to others what the Holy Spirit has taught me.

I am blessed to have special encouragers in my mother- by-marriage, Julia. It would be impossible to tell how much her love and belief in how my writing helps people means to me. Her sisters, Sarah, and Annelle, are some of the best distributors of the first book I know. Their belief in the helpfulness of the first book has been a tremendous encouragement and blessing.

Other people whose expertise have been of great benefit to me as a whole encouraged and cajoled me until I finally "got a move on" and finished this project. You know who you are.

Finally, my thanks to my family who "put up with me" and endure my shortcomings, who always think I can do and wait for me to get things done. Much love to Allen, Matt, Ben and Amber.

CONTENTS

COME FOLLOW GOD

Do You Want to Know God Personally?

Chapter 1: Following God personally through Prayer....................13

Chapter 2: Following God personally through Obedience 22

Chapter 3: Following God personally through Connection 28

Chapter 4: Following God Personally
 Through Remembering Who You Are 36

Chapter 5: Following God Personally Through Enhanced Faith ...42

INTRODUCTION

The confession of faith nearly everyone knows is "What is the whole duty of man(people)?" The expected answer is "to know Him and enjoy Him forever". I believe the other side of that question for God is "What is God's main aim for people?" The answer is "to know His people and to enjoy them forever". Through many years of walking with God, I have discovered He is very individually minded. The individual matters to God. God is the One who seeks out a person and issues an invitation to come to Him in belief and communion. God, through the Holy Spirit, places a longing into a person's mind and heart to search for Him. When that occurs, God will move Heaven and Earth to reach a person who sincerely wants to know the true God. He is also that way to a person who has a need to be helped in some way, or who has a question about God that needs an answer of any kind.

God wants to know you. He created Adam and Eve in order to have fellowship. In Genesis, we read God created the earth and everything that lives on the earth. He created day and night and the perfect conditions for the creations to live. He likes companionship so much that He decided to create someone who could communicate and fellowship with Him. Genesis 1: 24 *"Then God said, "Let Us make man in Our image, according to Our likeness…" VS 27: "So God created man in His own image; in the image of Gd He created him; male and female He created them.* "Created people came about because God wanted communication and fellowship of someone like Himself. Notice the "Us" in the narrative." Us" is the plural use of the word God. This speaks of the triune God; God the Father, God the Son and God the Holy Spirit.

In studying the Bible, I came across some information that seems to make sense to me concerning Adam's age when he disobeyed God and brought sin upon himself and humanity. I don't remember where I read this, but it seemed to make sense to me. Jesus is accepted to be 33 ½ years old when he died on the cross. Jesus is called the second "Adam". Quiet possibly Adam lived 33 ½ years before he ate the forbidden fruit. It seems reasonable to me that Adam, Eve, and God must have enjoyed fellowship for several years before that followship was jeopardized. Genesis 3:8 *"And they heard the sound of the LORD GOD walking in the garden in the cool of the day, and Adam and his wife hid themselves from the presence of the LORD GOD among the trees of the garden.* Evidently an afternoon fellowship time was not unusual. Probably Adam and Eve excitedly ran to meet God eager to be with Him. That time they did not run to meet Him. God knew the reason, but they had to confess their sin. Fellowship with God's prized creation had been broken forever. God took it upon Himself to make a way to bridge the enormous gap.

When I was growing up, I used to hear people who had a firm conviction about something that was threatened say, "If that happens it will be over my dead body". Think about this. Since sin came into the life of humankind, in reality God and people lost fellowship and communion forever. God was not willing to be separated from people forever. He had enjoyed His daily walks with Adam and Eve. He did not want to lose His new creation who resulted in fellowship and communion. Then it was as if He said, "losing this blessing will be over my dead body". God came in the person of Jesus and died in order to bridge the gap between God and people. The great part about His plan to restore, was even though Jesus died, He did not stay dead. He rose from death to live eternally. God's plan worked. Today we can have fellowship and communion with God. We can know Him and enjoy Him. God can know you and enjoy being with you.

God seeks out and calls a person to come to Him in belief while rejecting the old ways of forgetting God. This book is an attempt to share with you, the reader, some of my own experiences about getting to know God and learning to follow Him.

CHAPTER 1

Following God personally through <u>Prayer</u>

"Could I really ask God that?" You are not the only person to ask me that question. Believers have many questions in common. The problem lies in not knowing God as a person who is close to you. He is a personal God. This is one of the main differences you will find when you study other world religions or sects.

In getting to know God, first learn to pray. Think about what prayer really is. Prayer is a request to God in the name of Jesus facilitated by the Holy Spirit. A person learns to pray by studying the Bible's prayers. Read the prayers of devoted people in the Bible. Read what Jesus said about prayer. Then take God at His word. In first instances of learning to pray, you may want to pray the familiar prayers. It really helps to pray by following Jesus' example. Matthew 6: 9-13 *"In this manner, therefore, pray: Our Father in heaven, hallowed be your name. Your kingdom come. Your will be done on earth as it is in heaven. Give us this day our daily bread. And forgive us our debtors. And do not lead us into temptation. But deliver us from the evil one. For Yours is the kingdom and the power and the glory forever. Amen."*

Going into God's presence first with a smile of praise and thanksgiving sets a better tone for fellowship than running in with the frown of "O, me, my sin is so terrible". Remember always you have the right and privilege to go to God any time. Think about a good father who is always glad to see his child run to greet him. That is the picture to have in your mind when you approach our Father God.

One night my husband and I went to a visitation at a funeral home because a friend's mother had died. While we were visiting with our friends, his newly married daughter came to him and asked for 50 cents for the coke machine. Clayton reached in his pocket and gave her 50 cents. I wondered why she asked her father for money for a coke instead of her new husband. Pondering on this question made me think of God. Jesus said something interesting about asking for something. In Matthew 7: 8-9, He said, "Ask, *and it will be given to you; seek, and you will find; knock, and it will be opened to you. For everyone who asks receives, and he who seeks finds, and to him who knocks it will be opened."*

These thoughts came to mind: 1.) She knew she could go to her father. 2.) She knew he had what she wanted. And 3.) She knew he would give her what she asked. What an accurate picture of our Heavenly Father! Our Father God likes for his children to act like children. Never think you are "bothering" God when you have a need or a deeply felt want. I think God is probably grieved because so many times people think "I couldn't ask God that".

Please do not misunderstand me. I am not advocating being frivolous about prayers. Remember what I said about learning to pray? We learn to pray the same way we get to know a person who becomes our friend. To become a friend, we spend time with a person, we share interests, we share joys and sorrows. Over a period of time a good relationship develops. That friend becomes one who stands by you in your joys and in your sorrows. You know you can depend on that friend to help you with anything and to go with you through anything. Getting to know God personally is like that.

Growing in learning to pray comes about in stages and levels of difficulty of adventuring out in prayer as your faith in Him grows. First, you may pray simple prayers. Then as you realize God is responding to your prayers, venture out in belief and expand your conversations with Him. The main aspect of prayer is to be specific. What do you want God to do? What is your need? What do you want? Tell Him that. God can't demonstrate His answer to a generality. You will not know God has answered a general request. Something like, 'God bless the family down the road,' results in not knowing if you got an answer. A prayer for a definite need for the family is like 'Lord, Mr. Brown needs a job right away' will be answered, you will know it when he gets the job, then you can praise God for the answer. See the difference? Prayer activates God's power. God has ordained that prayer be the means by which we receive from Him. Watchman Nee wrote: "Prayer is the railroad tracks that God's train (power) runs on." If Christians don't "lay tracks", then God's train cannot run there. What a responsibility!

I would like to share some of my extraordinary prayers and their extraordinary answers. These are prayers I want to share with you because they are prime examples of how much God cares about the life of an individual believer. I am an ordinary believer who takes God at His Word. If the Word of God isn't appropriate for me today, if His instructions are not useful today, then what value does the Bible have for me and others? So, I will trust and act on His Word and see what happens. I have never been disappointed. His answers to these prayers and many others have strengthened my faith and enabled me to help other people. If you will exercise belief and trust in God you will not be disappointed either.

Graduation from High School is an event that all of us look forward to with anticipation and a little apprehension. In my home county, there are two Junior Colleges. The one most attended is Jones County Junior College. Southeastern Junior College is a private college which offers Bible courses.

My Uncle Ott and Aunt Alta gave me a book for graduation which made a deep impression on my life and the decisions I would make during my life. That book was <u>What Would Jesus Do?</u> Written by Charles Sheldon, that book has blessed many people. Mother and most of my relatives wanted me to attend Jones County Junior College. Mother and I went to Jones County Junior College and I chose my classes and the schedule for the first semester. My heart was so troubled. What would Jesus do? He would go to Southeastern. I was so miserable. Finally, I told my mother about the conflict in my spirit. I had prayed and asked God to make it possible for me to go to Southeastern. When I approached her about switching colleges, she was very upset. Taking a deep breath and saying my SOS prayer, "LORD, help", I made a deal with her. If I can get the same classes at Southeastern that I'm enrolled in at J.C., would you let me go to Southeastern? We went to investigate the courses at Southeastern. Not only could I get the same courses, but also Bible courses were available. Mother reluctantly agreed. I canceled the enrollment at J.C. and finished two years at Southeastern with two years of Old Testament and New Testament Studies. Those Bible courses have been the foundation of my years of Bible Study and over fifty years of Bible Teaching and writing. God demonstrated His love and His will for a shy 17-year-old girl.

A very interesting part concerning God's answers to prayer is He rarely sends just one side of an answer. Since I attended and graduated from Southeastern, it was not a question for my brother who followed me. Larry enrolled after high school, signed up for the courses he needed, and was on the basketball team which he enjoyed. Because of the good foundation he received in Bible studies, he has gone on to be a Bible Teacher as well, and has been teaching Sunday School in the churches where his membership has been.

Before I proceed to tell you about some other prayer answers, you need to understand God is not to be used like a gumball machine__ put in a nickel and get your piece of gum. God teaches a person about trusting Him and about believing His Word. The Bible has many instructions concerning obeying and trusting Him. As you read the Bible, take its truths to heart and believe, acting on God's Word demonstrates faith. Faith is honored by God.

In the beginning of exercising faith, God will probably show up in such a definite way, you will be almost mystified. As you continually exercise faith in actions and in prayer, fellowship may change. A change in the manner of fellowship demonstrates growth. As a person grows in faith, it may seem sometimes as if God does not hear. Do not be discouraged. If God trusts you with a silence, that is a big compliment! Faith grows by using faith. It seems that faith grows by exercising it. God encourages a person to stretch faith as far as you can think in order to see what He will do for you.

The next big crisis to come into my life was in my senior year at the University of Southern Mississippi. My major in Home Economics required a semester of living in a Home Management House. Home Economics majors had to spend a semester in one of the two houses belonging to the Department. Six girls would live in each house and perform duties according to a rotation schedule. My last semester I went to the meeting to determine which house I would live in and which duty would be my first assignment. To determine which house a student lived in, and the structure of assignments, we drew pieces of paper from baskets. That drawing determined which house, which roommate, which bedroom and which first duty in the rotation a student was assigned. On the day the twelve girls met for this important assignment, I was nervous. I did not know any of the other girls who were also sharing this very important course. My draw assigned me to the Kate Hubbard House.

Marianna Albritton

During the first week of the Home Management Course, I suffered an injury that made it impossible to fulfill the duties of that course. I had to withdraw from the Home Management House course and would have to fulfill that course the next semester.

The next semester came with a certain dread. I had to take the Home Management Course in order to fulfill the requirements of a degree in Home Economics. On the day we were to draw for our assignments, I went to a private place to pray. My nerves were like melting jello. I was almost literally shaking. My prayer was this:" Dear God, you know how I feel. I am so scared. Would you let me get in the Grace Bennett House? Would you please make sure my best friend Mary Nell gets in the same house? Thank you. Amen".

Upon arriving at the meeting, I found Mary Nell already there. She knew how nervous I was. One of our teachers was there with the baskets holding those important pieces of paper. At 2:00 p.m., twelve girls awaited the results those baskets and their pieces of paper would have on their lives. The basket was passed around for the twelve girls to draw a piece of paper revealing which house would be their assignment. Mary Nell drew a piece of paper. The paper read —Grace Bennett House. My piece of paper read— Grace Bennett House. Oh, how relieved I felt! The next paper was for the bedroom assignment. Mary Nell drew a paper reading the downstairs front bedroom. (Incidentally, that was the best bedroom in the house.) I drew a piece of paper. It read—downstairs front bedroom. That meant that not only would Mary Nell and I would be in the same house, but that we would be roommates. The last paper was drawn for first duties. You have probably guessed by now. We were Cook and Assistant Cook. My heart was beating so fast. This time not out of fear and nervousness, but of praise and thanksgiving to God.

Everyone in the room was amazed. The teacher said in the history of the Home Management House, such a thing as best friends being in the same house and having these results had never happened. She told us since she knew it was impossible to cheat or rig this, she would let it stand. But she was not pleased. No one could understand how this could happen.

When Mary Nell and I got outside and away from other people, she looked at me and said, "How did that happen?" I told her about my prayer and explained that God answered that prayer even better than I asked. When one of God's children is in a crisis, He will help. He may even answer in a way totally amazing. Ephesians 3: 20-21 *"Now to Him who is able to do exceedingly abundantly above all that we ask or think, according to the power that works in us to Him be glory in the church by Christ Jesus to all generations, forever and ever. Amen"*

So, on the appointed day, the six girls assigned to the Grace Bennett House reported for duty. God takes all possibilities into account when He answers prayer, in two weeks we would find out how much God's intervention would mean to us. Mary Nell caught pneumonia from the air conditioning in our bedroom. There were no blankets in our room. Her bed was located where the air conditioning vent blew directly on her. My friend from church came to the rescue. She brought us two army blankets to use during the rest of our stay in the House. Since Mary Nell was sick, and could only manage to go to class, I did her duty and mine until she was well. We managed to keep that a secret so she would not be forced to leave the Home Management House.

Unless you have been a Home Economics major with the curriculum required, it is not possible to know how stressful that particular course is. I do not think I could have completed the course requirements if God has not intervened so powerfully to help when it became overwhelming. Mary Nell and I both graduated with a B.S. degree in Home Economics. I went on to teach Home Economics in high school and she became an extension agent with 4-H clubs.

This experience resulted in a spiritual growth leap. God's Word encourages people to read about His promises and act upon them.

Promises found in God's Word still apply today, tomorrow, and forever. Whatever God had written in the Bible stands forever. Isaiah 40: 8 *"The grass withers, the flower fades, but the Word of our God stands forever"*. The Word of God illustrates if a person acts on a particular verse in the Bible, believing He will truly act, God will honor His Word. This is the truth moment for Christians. Will I act on a situation by choosing to believe God and be so bold as to pray an "extraordinary" prayer? Will I go out 'on a limb' and pray a prayer some people may think is 'crazy'? Praying with this kind of intensity yields amazing answers. Prayers yielding not only extraordinary answers, but also the building of faith and comfort in fellowship. Knowing that God is indeed really interested in the individual and is willing to be present in and with an individual is the result of "stretching" faith. God will let a person know Him as much as a person wants to know Him. He is a gentleman and does not force Himself nor His fellowship on anyone. He will go as far in getting to know you as you want to know Him.

A barrier to stepping out to get to know God on a personal basis is the same barrier that came between Adam and Eve and their fellowship with God: fear. Unwarranted fear. Some Bible Study students have asked me "What will God make me do if I surrender completely to Him"? Why do people think the worst of God? Why are people so afraid to fully surrender to God? I think it is because the same fear the enemy of the soul placed in Adam and Eve's mind is the same fear that comes into the mind of people even today. That oppressing fear is a thought. This thought is "God is not being good to you. He may not do the best for you." This same lie has been perpetrated by the enemy since the Garden of Eden. This lie has stopped too many people from getting to really know Jesus. Please do not accept this lie. God only wants good for you. Jeremiah 29: 11 *"For I know the thoughts that I think toward you, says the LORD, thoughts of peace and not of evil, to give you a future and a hope."* Believe God.

Come Follow God

Do not be afraid to pray about anything that concerns you or your family and friends. After marrying Allen, his job with Masonite Corporation, moved us to Lucedale, Mississippi. He soon became good friends with Clayton and his son Chuck. The three of them liked to deer hunt. On the opening day of deer season one year, Allen was concerned about the location Clayton wanted to hunt. He wanted to go to a place called Leaf Pasture. Allen said a lot of people liked to hunt there on the first day of hunting season. He was worried the woods would be too crowded. The morning arrived and they left to go to Leaf Pasture. I went to pray. "Lord, Allen is worried about this place to hunt today. Please take care of Allen, Clayton, and Chuck." A question came to my mind. "What are you afraid of?" I said, "Stray bullets". Then peace came and I went about my day. After dark, Allen returned from the hunt. I asked him how the hunt went. He reported no one got a deer. But an interesting thing had happened. I asked "what?" He said, "There was not anyone in the woods but us". I didn't tell him about that prayer. The Lord and I had a big smile together. Well, I suppose he knows about the prayer now.

CHAPTER 2

Following God personally through <u>Obedience</u>

Getting to know God as you know your friend beside you, involves interaction with Him. Reading the Bible consistently is essential to knowing God. As you read the Bible, you will begin to see how the verses meet your needs of the moment. Many times, as you have a question or have a need, the Holy Spirit will guide you to the exact verse or verses you need. When this happens, it increases your faith. To see an example like this is a thrill to your soul. You will really understand the importance of obedience. As human beings, we tend to rebel against obedience. This comes as a result of the disobedience in the Garden of Eden. Obedience is a battle. Fight the tendency to rebel against obedience.

God will lead you to carry out "assignments". At times, these assignments may seem foolish, possibly having the potential for embarrassment, or just seem odd. These examples are for the purpose of learning obedience and direction. (Just for the record, none of my assignments have caused any negative results.) People tend to think the worst when it comes to acting "outside of the box".

Obedience for most of us, I think, is a scary word. The Bible describes obedience as better than sacrifice. 1Samuel 15: 22c *"…Behold, to obey is better than sacrifice."* To sacrifice means giving up my own self desire. This results in symbolizing some kind of service to God. Sometimes we may rather do a service of some kind to substitute for obedience.

Christians are advised to obey God's directions to pray and read the Bible. These are the beginnings of obedience. As a Christian grows spiritually, God often by the Holy Spirit places a thought in the mind to obey. He starts this learning process slowly and easily. Great blessing awaits if a person takes heed and follows through.

One way God trains us to obey is to place a particular person on our mind. As this person's name keeps occurring to us, call that person for a chat. Soon the person will mention some concern or problem. From that reference you will know how to pray for the exact problem or need. You and the person will be glad you called. When this first occurred with me, I thought "what if they think it strange, I called?" Never mind the questioning thoughts, follow the direction anyway. You will find out why you needed to call. It may have been the person was feeling a little down that day and needed to know the encouragement of a friend.

After you become comfortable with this kind of direction from the Holy Spirit, He will move up to another category of obedience. He may lead you to send a card to someone to just say 'I'm thinking of you'. He may lead you to give a certain amount of money to someone. (This is a hard one for me.)

One Thanksgiving week I was shopping for the items I needed to cook the Thanksgiving meal. I saw our Pastor's wife on the same grocery isle. The thought came into my mind, 'give her $25.00'. Many negative thoughts went through my mind, but I overcame them and walked up to her and said "I feel impressed to give you this money". She looked at the amount and said, "I wondered how I was going to be able to buy a turkey". How relieved I was not to have made a wrong move either way! She was blessed to be able to buy a turkey for Thanksgiving and I was blessed by feeling that God was pleased with me.

Another time this happened, we had a visiting preacher who had just launched his evangelism ministry. When the church service ended, the impression came to give him $20.00 as I shook hands with him as we left the church. He looked puzzled but thanked me. A week later, I got a letter from his wife. She said her Sunday School Class was sponsoring a refugee family and she didn't have any extra money. She reported that she was able to buy two bags of groceries for the family with that $20.00. Her happiness exploded in my soul. She must have been a very savvy shopper. I would like to know how she bought two bags of groceries with $20.00! However, that happened in the 1980's. Even then on our salaries, grocery bills seemed high.

God will lead you to opportunities to serve Him in ways that are particular to your spiritual gifts and your abilities. If God leads you to engage in service, He has already equipped you for that service. Thrust Him. He has done all the preparatory work in you.

When I was in Junior College, the Sunday School nomination committee asked me to teach the Junior High Sunday School class. I was used to being in a class not teaching a class. Being shy and bashful, such an idea seemed impossible for me. The chairman of the committee reminded me I was taking Bible at Southeastern and the committee believed I could teach the class. There I was, face to face with a choice to obey God's plan or back away. Always say "yes" to God. So, saying yes to the committee, I began teaching my first Sunday School Class. Agreeing to follow God and depend on Him to do what I could not do myself, there has never been a time I've regretted that obedience.

Come Follow God

After my time at Southeastern ended, I enrolled at the University of Southern Mississippi. That was a somewhat frightening experience. Having never been away from home for more than a week, that was a difficult adjustment in many ways. Still determined to follow God in all my ways, my prayer was the same— "LORD, do for me what I cannot do for myself". Using the thought "What would Jesus do?" as a guide for making decisions, I went through each day.

To my surprise, and complete amazement, girls in my dorm started coming to me with questions and personal problems. To the best of my ability to follow God's directions, I did the best to give godly solutions and answers to them. Obedience leads in interesting directions!

One incident really surprised me. There was one girl on my floor in the first dorm I lived in who would come to the room and begin a conversation in which she would criticize believers in Jesus and condemn religion. I didn't argue with her. I just stated my belief in Jesus. Very early one morning, I heard a knock on our door. I got up to open the door and there was that girl. She fainted and fell in my doorway! Calling for help, I wondered why she chose my door to knock on. I believe she came to my door because she was confident, she would be helped. A person never knows about the witness he/she is leaving with other people.

Many years later when my family had to make a third move to another city because of my husband's job change, I really wondered why God was moving us. I was teaching a Sunday School Class, teaching a Ladies' Bible Study Class and had an active counseling ministry with the Ladies in our Church. The lesson here? <u>Follow God whether you understand or not.</u>

One afternoon I was in the kitchen, feeling useless because I had no class to teach and no one to discuss the Scriptures with. I asked God, "Why am I here?" There are no neighbors close by and this new church doesn't know anything about me. He set me straight. "Learn of Me". Learn of God. What did He mean by that? This new job of Allen's put us 30 minutes in any direction we needed to drive. So, I had plenty of time to go to my new study (The house that went with the job was big and I could have a room for a study just for me.) So, I began to spend more time studying and writing Bible Studies.

We had been at Big Level Church about four months when the Chairman of the Sunday School Department asked me to teach a new Sunday School Class. They wanted to start a class for the ages 50-60. Well, I had never taught a class whose members were older than I was. This was another stretch. Saying "Yes" was another best thing I ever did in following God. What a wonderful experience! The privilege of teaching that class lasted 15 years. Then Allen's job changed again and we had to move.

During those 15 years, God lead me through other unimagined service opportunities. For example, individual discipling of one on one, teaching Bible Studies at other churches, and writing for the Baptist Sunday School board. When God said, "learn of Me" I had no idea what would be ahead. How fantastic! What blessing! God had brought me so far in fellowship and service. Never in my imagination would I have ever thought to have such wonderful opportunies to serve Him.

I asked my closest friend what her biggest stretch in following God has been. She has experienced two stretches she never imagined. At 70 years of age, God led her to go on a mission trip for the first time. She was thrilled to obey and go. And that was not her last mission trip. That mission trip opened up an opportunity she really never imagined. She has a wonderful singing voice and loves to sing in the church choir. Because of that mission trip, she met a man who leads The North Texas Singers who take cruises for missions. He asked her if she would consider joining their choir and go on mission cruises. It did not take her long to say "yes". She has been on four mission cruises and sang for more people than she ever imagined. See how following God in obedience is so full of joy? Following God is not a burden nor an imposition.

Before COVID-19 changed our lives, she felt God wanted her to help organize a new Sunday School Class for ladies who were not currently enrolled in a Sunday School Class. On the first Sunday they met, she ended up teaching the class. She told God, "I didn't mean to teach, I meant to organize the class." He impressed her mind with "it is not about what you want; it is about obedience". As a footnote, she really enjoys teaching the class.

CHAPTER 3

Following God personally through <u>Connection</u>

God is so pleased to get to know you personally, that He confirms His leadership through other believers. Encouragement from God gives incentive to act and to be involved with His actions and dealings with other believers. These occasions are precious and often surprising. To realize God has enough confidence in you to trust you to help someone to know Him, or to help someone find an answer to a question which has been bothering them, brings unspeakable joy and a sense of accomplishment nothing else can give. Following God becomes real in your life as you learn to pray boldly and honestly. Also, you must learn to obey instantly. This part of following God is very interesting. I cannot tell you how many times I have been impressed to study certain scriptures, and to pray to understand them as thoroughly as possible only to have someone ask me a question related to that exact study. The first time that happened I was so shocked it took a little while to respond. Now I am not shocked, but amazed and thankful when someone asks me a question, or seeks the answer to a spiritual problem.

An early example of this occurrence happened in a couples' Bible Study Class. A lady I did not know, stopped me as we were filing out of the class. She said, "God told me you could help me". Replying "OK", I wondered what God had in mind. Remember I said God prepares you in advance for any service you will need to give. She shared that she had committed a sin in her youth that still haunted her. She was in spiritual misery. Now, our Heavenly Father does not want His children to bare heavy burdens when Jesus came to take our sins and burdens upon Himself! I shared 1 John 1: 9 with her. *"If we confess our sins, He is faithful and just to forgive us our sins and to cleanse us from all unrighteousness"*. I listened as she told me about the heavy burden on her heart. The Holy Spirit brought to my mind the scriptures she needed. After she prayed and asked God to forgive that sin, I assured her that based on God's word she was forgiven and cleansed. Her spiritual condition before God now was such that she had not sinned. As some might like to say, God tossed that sin in His pond of forgiveness and put up a "No Fishing" sign. Sometimes people have a way of pulling up the remembrance of sin and punishing themselves over and over. Don't do it! Psalm 103:12 *"As far as the east is from the west, so far has He removed our transgressions from us."* We have God's word on His forgiveness. When God forgives us, who are we not to forgive ourselves?

I was attending the wake of my cousin's son. After greeting the family, I went to sit in an out of the way place. My elderly aunt, Alta came and sat down beside me. That was not unusual. We had always been close. Among all my aunts, she had done especially thoughtful things for me over the years and we shared Christian themed books. Therefore, I was glad for her presence at that time. To my complete shock she asked me, "Do you know what happens to us when we die?" Sending up my SOS prayer," LORD, help!" I replied, "Yes

Ma'am, I just studied that subject in my Bible study time". We found a secluded place in the lobby and I shared what I studied the week before that trip. Isn't God something! He knew what I studied. He knew what my aunt wanted to know. I copied all my notes on that subject and gave them to her the next day. Sometimes people are shy about asking questions. My aunt was married to a deacon in the church and her father had been a pastor. Either she had not thought of the question earlier in life or was hesitant to ask. This was the perfect timing for both of us. Not one person came near us while I was explaining my study to her. God protected our space and time as long as needed. What a joy to be trusted by God! And what a blessing to be able to help my dear aunt. I just love how God works on both sides of an issue and brings about the right meeting at the right time. This kind of event and its positive result has to be the greatest "high" there is!

"Knowing God personally through connections" is an awesome thought. How can I be connected personally to God? Any connection must have a beginning, a foundation, and a point of reference. Jesus' disciples asked Him to teach them how to pray. We talked a little about this in Chapter one. The only way to begin a connection to God is to pray. Jesus gave the disciples the model prayer we read in Matthew 6:9-13 "...*Our Father in heaven, hallowed be your name. Your kingdom come. Your will be done on earth as it is in heaven. Give us this day our daily bread. And forgive us our debts, as we forgive our debtors. And do not lead us into temptation, but deliver us from the evil one. For yours is the kingdom and the power and the glory forever. Amen.*"

Notice (1) the beginning is "our Father". Prayer is based on the basic relationship of child to father. When a person makes the choice to ask Jesus to be the Savior of one's life, meaning body, soul and spirit, then the Creator of all things, the almighty God becomes to a person the ultimate father. As we recognize God as our Father, then it must be evident how sacred, holy and above all

He is. This is the person to whom we pray. This Person, God, is the solitary power to whom we direct prayer. The first entry into prayer must be the recognition of who God is, and the recognition of His amazing being.

This recognition is important because everything else is dependent upon this fact. Through observation, I have heard people begin to ask forgiveness for sins or ask for help, needs, wants etc. and not stop first to get into a proper attitude of being in God's presence. Follow the model.

Notice (2) the foundation of priority. The priority of the recognition of God is His kingdom and its arrival. Be mindful of God's kingdom which has been since eternity, is now, and will come. God's heart wish is for His kingdom (His governance, His goodness, His provision) to rule on earth. God wants people who are His children to ask Him to bring His kingdom to earth in order for the very best there is to be our environment. The other part to asking for His will to be done on earth as it is in heaven applies to us. Pray for God's will to be done in you as His will is written in heaven for you (for we are earth also). This is a tremendous blessing. I believe this makes a big difference in my life. I have a prayer to cover as many areas of influence as possible: "Dear Father, your will, your way, your time, your purpose and your glory in my life. Amen"

Too many believers today, I think, are caught up in the here and now and don't really want to pray for God's kingdom to come because that will result in the change of life as we know it. Faith is put to the test of priority. Most of the time life for us seems to be good and allows us to have good things. But there is much sorrow, danger, and distress around us. Wouldn't it be nice to have God's best with no sorrow, danger, nor distress! The problem with our thinking is we would rather have what we know, rather than have the absolute best we do not know.

Could we not pray for God's kingdom to come on earth and His will to be done on earth just like it is in heaven until we really begin to desire this? Such prayers will please God very much.

Notice (3) the reference point of the boundary stake. In land surveying, there is a beginning point of reference known as the boundary stake. Accurate land survey starts there and from there proceeds the boundaries of land ownership. Notice that God's ownership begins and ends with a definite time and place.

Requests for needs and wants are included within the boundary of the first and last acknowledgements. Respect for God and acknowledgement of the truth of His being is the beginning, the foundation is to want what God wants and the reference point is to realize the reality of His boundaries. We may then ask for wants, needs, forgiveness, second chances etc. God wants to give us what we need. He even desires to give us what we want many times. Some cases in point, I have shared with you already. Everything a person can think of to pray about is dependent on God's power, His rulership (kingdom), and the fact of His glory. Glory means "weight". Only God has the optimum weight behind words and actions to accomplish anything at all. God is the only person who can do anything about anything at all. He alone has all power and all ability.

In the early years of space exploration, I personally knew people who did not believe men were sent into space. When a man landed on the moon and planted the United States flag, one of my Daddy's employees said that was filmed in a desert. He did not believe a man could go to the moon and walk around. Just because he did not believe a man went to the moon did not make the action untrue. In today's time frame there are people who do not believe God exists with all His power and knowledge. That unbelief does not make God nonexistent. Unbelief does not change truth.

Hugh Ross says the further a person gets from nature, the less likely they are to believe in God. I think he is correct. Being connected to nature allows people to see God's hand work, to see how nature flows together in its existence, and to see how life and death plays out. In a concrete surrounded world, it would be hard to see how one thing may relate to or be dependent on another. The habits and mannerisms of wildlife go unnoticed if you are not there to see them. God teaches many lessons through the example of interactions between people and animals, birds and plant life. By observation of God's designs in creation, it has been a delight to me to see how many times God uses the same designs in many differing forms of nature. Just recently, I saw a high-resolution picture of some islands in one of the oceans. They were small, uninhabited islands. Looking at them, they were in the shape of, and looked like leaves with stems. Look at the shape of a snail. You will see that design repeated in nature many times. This is just two examples. You might enjoy looking for more repeated designs of other kinds found in nature.

Connection through action proves solidarity. As my husband, hoes the garden, he flips out worms and grubs to a certain mockingbird who has taken to following him as he works in the garden. The bird never fusses at Allen and is content to stay near him. But, if someone else or one of our pets get close to the bird, it raises a fuss. The bird has made a connection to Allen with provision. It realizes Allen is a help, not a source of harm. When people make a connection with God, they realize He is a help, not a source of harm.

I have given some scripture verses related to prayer. Scripture verses help us connect to God. Have you ever realized how Psalm 100 will help you connect to God? This Psalm pictures the floor plan of the Tabernacle in the wilderness. First, a person had to go through a gate. Second, the gate led to the courtyard. Third, only the High Priest could go into the Most Holy Place into God's presence. Today because Jesus has placed His blood on the Mercy Seat in the Most

Holy Place in heaven everyone who believes in Jesus as Savior has access to the presence of God.

Psalm 100: 4a *"Enter His gates with thanksgiving".* Picture yourself following this order of prayer. Enter His gate with giving of thanks for the blessings you have received from Him. Think about how thanks are different from praises. Giving thanks has to do with God's acts. Praise has to do with God's attributes. Psalm 100: 4b *"And into His courts with praise".* See how you are progressing through God's dwelling? Now think of all the reasons to praise God for who He is. And then the desired place to be is in His presence. Psalm 100: 2b *"Come before His presence with singing."* Sing out loud the songs that come to your mind. Sing as long as you think of songs. Then, pray. You will be in God's presence and you will know it. You do not have to pray like this every time you pray, but this gives you a great connection for future prayer times.

God will connect you with people who need prayer, people who will be a good prayer partner for you, and people who want a greater connection with the Heavenly Father. He brings this about in many ways. I met my helper in ministry because of a Sunday Night Bible Study Class that only had two attendees. At the time, I started a class on the Tabernacle at night. There were several attendees. Garnet went to teach a class for new church members. Only one person came to her class. Since there was only one person, Garnet asked Amy if she would like to attend the Tabernacle study. So, they both came to my class. I had not met Garnet. She was looking for a prayer partner, and for some instruction on how to have a greater connection with Jesus. We became instant friends, and today she helps me in my ministry and is the go-to friend when I have a need of some kind. I try to be the same kind of friend to her.

Garnet had an experience recently when she was traveling. She went to sit in the hotel lobby by the fireplace. She had not been there long when a young lady came and sat in a chair near her. Soon they were in conversation when the lady opened up to Garnet about wanting to get to know Jesus. She felt she had not been able to find a way to Jesus. This time Garnet prayed the "SOS" prayer and began to tell her about her own experiences in finding Jesus to be real. The young lady listened intently. The next morning, she responded positively about the experience of their conversation. That is a real "Hallelujah"!

See how God does the connecting? Totally wonderful!

CHAPTER 4

Following God Personally <u>Through Remembering</u> <u>Who You Are</u>

A believer in Jesus as Savior changes a person into an adopted child of God. The very God who created and rules the universe becomes a father to you. Becoming a child of God through Jesus brings many blessings, but also many responsibilities. Remember this always: you belong to the family of God. Act accordingly. Being a child of God brings a major shift in how you see things, in how you treat people, and in your major life choices. Some students in my Bible Study classes ask me "How do I know what God wants me to do?" My answer is__ being a Christian is more about "being" than "doing". "Being" involves having your main focus on Jesus by means of prayer and studying the Bible." Being" means your focus is to make Jesus the most important person in your life.

Come Follow God

This is an everyday effort. Jesus does not mean for you to be rigid about your time. If employment or personal business obligations make it impossible to follow your regular prayer time, then that day as you go about your obligations, speak to Him in one sentence throughout the day as you would speak to a friend in passing or on a coffee break. In this way, you will come to have an easy flow of conversation and one day will notice that you have a relationship with Jesus you never expected to have.

"Doing" follows being. When we "be" His person, He chooses our assignments and activities. When we become a child of God, His Holy Spirit gives us a spiritual gift. This gift is chosen by Him. I guarantee you it will be good and you will enjoy using the gift for His service and the service of other people. You will probably be surprised by the gift He purposes for you. After all, He knows you better than you know yourself.

You have a new family relationship now. 2 Corinthians 6: 18 *"I will be a Father to you, and you shall be my sons and daughters, says the LORD Almighty."* Some people have/had a good father and therefore can identify God as such. Unfortunately, some earthly fathers are not good examples. Either example a person has been exposed to in life, can at least be used to form an idealized view of what a good father is.

I was blessed to have a good father. He not only provided the necessary things in life like food, clothing, and shelter, but also went the second mile for my brother and me in many ways. I could confidently "volunteer" my Daddy for school trips or school projects. He was always willing to do whatever my brother or I needed done concerning our school, boy scout, or 4-H club activities.

Remember you are who you are because of God's forgiveness. Ephesians 1:7 *"In Him we have redemption through His blood, the forgiveness of sins, according to the riches of His grace".* In every person, there is a hole in the soul which aches to be filled. People search for a way to fill that hole, but do so in vain until they meet Jesus and accept Him as their personal Savior. This is a difficult search for many. There are so many "voices" in the world that seek to pull people in all directions. Yet, when a person tries a false way, disillusionment fills the soul instead of peace and satisfaction. Here I need to insert a warning. If a person rejects the truth of Jesus Christ, God will let him/her follow a lie. That rejection will lead to a dangerous way and sometimes destruction.

My heart hurts for people who reject the truth and follow a lie. The truth in Jesus is so easy and so simple. There is something in the soul that wants to have a part in doing something to save themselves. This stumbling block is a kind of pride. People want to have Jesus plus "my efforts". It seems so hard for someone to understand and accept that Jesus has done everything needed for one's salvation.

I have noticed that some people want to judge God and come up with justifications for rejecting Him. Why do people think judging God and coming up with a belief system to suit themselves will be alright? Please stop and think! If Christians witnessing to the saving grace of God, are correct, then we have everything to gain. If we were to be wrong in our convictions, we would have nothing to lose. (I reached this conclusion after studying many belief systems.)

One of my cousins asked, "Is that all I have to do? Just believe in Jesus to forgive me?" Yes. Just believe in Jesus to save you. When a person asks Jesus to save, repentance is included because in asking Jesus for forgiveness a person is turning away from the previous life. Turning toward Jesus includes humility and surrender to someone greater than self. Notice this verse reads *forgiveness of sins according to the riches of His grace*. "According to" means a lot more than "out of". According to means giving a lot more. If someone had billions of dollars, and gave a person $1,000,000 that is according to. If a person had $1,000,000 and gave $100.00, that is out of.

Knowing I have forgiveness is very freeing. This takes away a lot of fear and anxiety concerning the future. Because I have been forgiven of sin I can pray, approaching The Very God as my Father. Hebrews 4: 16 *"Let us therefore come boldly to the throne of grace, that we may obtain mercy and find grace to help in time of need."* Grace means unlooked for and undeserved favor. Just think! I don't deserve the favor of God, but He rejoices to extend it to me. Remembering the example, God has whatever we may need or even want, but also, He has the ability and means to give.

The next aspect we need to know and keep in mind is that God gives us a Personal Assistant as well as a Savior. Most people know about God and Jesus, but the Holy Spirit is not as well known. He is the third person of the triunity. GOD is the Father; Jesus is the Son; and the Holy Spirit is the part of God who lives in us who guides us who believe in Him. I cannot come near to understanding The Triunity. However, I experience Him in all three parts of His Being. When He created people as recorded in Genesis 1: 2 "Then *God said, 'Let us make man in* Our *image, according to Our likeness;"* He made us a triunity. After His image which He speaks of in the plural, we are a body, a soul, and a spirit. The great difference is we cannot separate ourselves into only a body, a soul nor a spirit. GOD did that and continues to do that today. One GOD who can manifest as Father, Son, and Spirit loves every person so much He made a way to be a very personal God to the people He created. This is a truly amazing reality. John 3: 17 *"For God did not send His Son into the world to condemn the world, but that the world through Him might be saved."*

The Holy Spirit is the seal of God's living in us who believe in Jesus as Savior. What is the significance of a seal? A seal has several applications. A seal is a sign of ownership. A seal is a sign of authority. A seal is a sign of preservation. A seal is a sign of approval. A seal is a sign of authenticity. Realize God's seal is on believers for all these purposes. 2 Corinthians 1: 21-22 *"Now He who establishes us with you in Christ and has anointed us is God, who also has sealed us and given us the Spirit in our hearts as a guarantee."* It is impossible for God to forget me or you.

Marianna Albritton

Wouldn't it be great to have someone who always stands up for you? Well, you do. In coming to know God through remembering who you are, this is another blessing. 1 John 2: 1c "...*we have an Advocate with the Father, Jesus Christ the righteous.* An advocate is someone who defends you, supports you and takes up your cause. No matter what happens in a believer's life, one can go to Jesus for help, understanding, and solace. He will be willing to come to your aid. You may have to wait while He works out details and works in people's lives. He will stand beside you at all times.

Twenty-three years ago, my husband's job came to an end again. He had been employed by two good companies. Both of the companies decided to sell. We were in our 50's. This is not a good age to be without a job. His job had included a house for us to live in. So, we did not own a house of our own. Since our sons were in school during the years he worked there, I did not work outside the home for several reasons. Actually, I helped him. His boss called me the "official unofficial secretary". My help was really needed in order for the business to work at its best. The work place and residence were 20 miles in one direction to anywhere. That distance meant most of my salary if I went to work would go for transportation, so I stayed home and worked for the company as needed.

When that job ended, our sons had finished high school and were then in college. My husband did get a new job. It meant we had to move to another county in Mississippi. And his salary was lower than the previous job. We had to find a way to buy a house, and I had not worked as a teacher in 25 years. The scenario did not look good. You can imagine how much praying was done during that time!

One day as I was sending off the bills, I discovered there was not enough money to pay all the bills. Discouragement set in. We were in the worst condition we had been in a long time. As I prayed, King Hezekiah's prayer came to mind and I stopped and read 2 Kings 19: 14-20. Like King Hezekiah, I laid the checkbook and the bills before the LORD and prayed to Him to work out this situation. The next day the George County High School Principal called me and asked if I could go for a job interview. The next day I had a job teaching Spanish. Marianna, remember who you are.

After not working in the public for 25 years, and being 50 years of age, I got a job teaching school again and we were able to buy a house. God also made sure we were able to get loans and help our sons finish college. (They were both in college at the same time.)

Come to know God through remembering who you are in Him. You are a child of God, You are forgiven, you have the Holy Spirit living in you, You have God's seal on you, and you have the best advocate possible. There is nothing good He will not do for you. You can depend on Him. During difficult times, it is easy to forget whose you are. Stop. Get your soul's compass pointed in the right direction. Remember who you are in Jesus.

CHAPTER 5

Following God Personally Through <u>Enhanced Faith</u>

The previously mentioned steps of growth in following God naturally cause an increase of faith and an ability to stay connected with God whatever circumstances happen in a believer's life. An added bonus to this process will without doubt cause God to give a "well done" response to the one who determines to follow God and know Him personally. Knowing that sense of God's pleasure in fellowship with God is very fulfilling.

By now you are probably trying to put all you've read together in your mind to begin your understanding of growing in desire to know, follow and have a real relationship with God through Jesus under the leadership of the Holy Spirit. Just start the following God process in small steps. Your fellowship will grow bit by bit and sometimes rather rapidly.

God develops faith through a process. The process of one lesson at a time. Isaiah 28: 10 *"For precept must be upon precept, precept upon precept, line upon line, line upon line, here a little, there a little."* Faith develops and grows deeper as a person has experiences in life. Handle the circumstances in your life with confidence in God. He comes in to help only with your permission. Isn't it awesome that God with all His power will not intrude in your life, but will only come if you want His participation? You can have as good a relationship with God as you want. You will never regret the effort you put into knowing Him. Sometimes it may take bulldog determination to keep going forward, because there is an enemy who would want to stop your growth. I have developed a question to ask myself when I encounter a problem: "Is this going to matter in eternity?"

From reading each chapter in this book you have found experiences with which to identify, experiences that have been similar to your own experiences, and hopefully something that will encourage you to step out in faith, more faith than ever exercised to stretch your growth. God seems to really enjoy giving you some "stretch" experiences to enhance your growth. Through faith you will accomplish something new in your service.

A new avenue of service will come to you which you may not ever have imagined yourself doing. In 1988, the pastor of a church on the Gulf Coast, called me to ask if I would speak one night during a Layman's Revival. Who me? What a stretch. I called a friend to go with me to pray me through my speech, and went. Oh, my! I never expected that.

Having enhanced faith enables you to step out and use your faith as a natural course of life's activities. Our older son, Matt, uses his faith naturally as a part of each day's activities whether in work, or recreation. His fellowship with Jesus resonates quietly and people easily gravitate to him when they have some kind of problem or question about God. He finds himself in a place where people open up to him unexpectedly. Because he follows the recommendation to always be ready to give a reason for your faith, he blesses other people with an answer to problems, questions, and prayer needs. 1 Peter 3:

15 *'...and always be ready to give a defense to everyone who asks you a reason for the hope that is in you..."*

One day while he was making a regular inspection appointment, he found the secretary in tears. Because he had worked with her for a number of years, he felt it would be alright to ask her what was wrong. She replied her husband had just called to tell her he had just been fired from his job in a pharmacy. The reason he was fired? A customer asked him about his faith in Jesus and the pharmacist talked to the customer about how he could know Jesus as Savior. The store fired him for talking about Jesus on the job.

Matt told her God can handle any problem and especially will help when the problem involves a person trying to live for God. He told her that he would pray, and call me to help them pray for her husband to get a new job soon. She was comforted by Matt's belief God would help them. In two weeks, the pharmacist had a new job in a store that not only hired him, but made him the manager of their pharmacy and gave him a raise! Hey, God does all thing well!

These kinds of things happen to Matt all the time. Why? Because quiet deep-down faith in God shines through. Loudly vocal and insistent witnessing for God usually turns people off to listening. But, when people "see" someone who has the Holy Spirit's leadership governing a life, they will gravitate to real faith.

Faith is the life-giving, building particle of Christian life. Ephesians 2: 8 *"For by grace you have been saved through faith, and that not of yourselves; it is the gift of God"*. Faith is the means by which we can be saved. We do not even have to muster up the needed faith. That faith is given to us by God.

God gives us the first installment of faith to be saved through, and we must follow to keep making that faith grow. Romans 10: 17 *"So then faith comes by hearing, and hearing by the word of God."* Keep in mind the Word of God is the Bible. In order for faith to grow into enhanced faith, Bible study is needed. Since faith cannot be seen, touched, nor felt, you have to reach out and use faith as an unseen element. As exercise builds physical muscles, using faith builds spiritual muscles. As you have read in this book in previous chapters, reading the Bible gives the courage to exercise faith. You know what to do because you read something in the Scripture. You know how to pray because of the encouragement to pray you read in the scriptures, and examples of prayer found in the scriptures.

In order to pray, you need to read the Bible. In order to read the Bible, you need to pray. These are two intertwined necessities of the Christian life. I like to read this verse before I study the Bible. Luke 24: 45 *"And He opened their understanding, that they might comprehend the Scriptures."* Jesus opened the disciples' understanding as they read the Scriptures. The only way to properly understand God's Word is for Him to open our understanding. Without this we cannot properly understand and may even distort the meaning. Be serious in your study of the Bible. Get a good Bible concordance so you can look up other verses that relate to what you are studying. And, do your best to get a good commentary. I recommend <u>The Bible Exposition Commentary</u> by Warren W. Wiersbe. This is an inexpensive two volume commentary on the New Testament. Also, I enjoy using The David Jeremiah Study Bible.

In other chapters, I have written about prayer. One prayer help I've recently discovered is the Jewish Tallit or Prayer Shawl. When the New Testament speaks of "going into your closet" to pray, this refers to using a prayer shawl when you pray. You cover your head and face in a shawl. This makes a "closet". It is really interesting to find how much this removes so many distractions and how much easier it is to pray this way. In reading about Susanna Wesley, the mother of John Wesley, it was interesting to find that she put her apron over her face and head when she prayed. She had so many children it was hard to have a private place. Everyone knew "when Mother puts her apron over her head, leave her alone." I don't know if she knew about the tallit or not, but she knew how to make a closet in which to pray.

Enhanced faith is going to be needed in the days to come. As current thought around the subject of faith in the one true God, the LORD Jesus Christ, seems to be slowly but surely coming under attack in several ways, we must have our feet firmly planted in faith in Him. I don't understand the rapid deceleration in belief in God, nor the sudden rise in vandalism of churches and religious monuments.

I understand the effect Covid has had on the ability to gather and worship, carry on youth activities, and have church fellowships, but I cannot understand how this short void has given rise to such a negativity to honoring God. I suppose the void has allowed anti-God people to have the space to express their ideas more.

Contributing to the mentioned negativity today, may be the influence of the many more religious ideas available during this time in history. People without a proper witness to becoming right with God through Jesus, are confused, I think. The sad result of this situation is a person who chooses a false belief system. When a person rejects The Way, The Truth, and The Life, following a false way comes next. John 14: 6 *"Jesus said to him, I am the way, the truth, and the life, No one comes to the Father except through Me."* Sadly, we have observed false leaders arise who seem to be the very thing some people are looking for. Unfortunately, we have seen those false leaders sink deeper and deeper into leading their followers into sin which ultimately cannot bring peace into a life. Tragic outcomes have been the result in a lot of cases.

Keep your faith in God. Jesus never fails. The way to God is simple. Ask God to show you the truth about Himself. He will lead you to the truth.

Finding Jesus as Savior is as easy as A, B, C.

ASK. Ask Jesus to come into your life. Romans 10: 13 "For *whosoever calls on the name of the LORD shall be saved."*

Come Follow God

BELIEVE. Simply believe Jesus paid the complete price for your salvation. Romans 10: 10 *"For with the heart one believes unto righteousness, and with the mouth confession is made unto salvation."*

CONFESS. Confess means to agree with God that you need Him to do for you that which you cannot do for yourself. Romans 10: 9 *"that if you confess with your mouth the Lord Jesus and believe in your heart that God has raised Him from the dead, you will be saved."*

Having done that, you will be saved (delivered from sin and its consequences). Some people get tripped up because eternal salvation is so easy for people to receive. But remember it was not easy for Jesus. Salvation is Jesus only, not Jesus plus something. There is not one thing a person can do to earn salvation, nor help Jesus in His role as Savior.

Now, whether you have been a believer for years, or have just now asked Jesus into your life, enhance your faith by continuing with Him.

COME FOLLOW GOD.

STUDY GUIDE

COME FOLLOW GOD

1. Find a place in your home to make your special place to pray and read the Bible.

2. Get a notebook to make notes about prayer and Bible reading each day. Some days your notes will be short. Other days you may write a page or more. Try to read Luke 24:45 each time before Bible reading.

3. Carry out "obedience" exercises as you receive them. Write about these in your notebook.

4. Look for God to place you with people who need prayer, need encouragement, or who need to know how Jesus has made a difference in your life.

5. If you have a present difficulty, ask the LORD to give you a Bible verse. Write down His answer in your notebook and date it. Problems, trials, and difficulties are overcome by the Word, the Blood, and the Holy Spirit working together for you. Because of the power of Jesus' blood, the Holy Spirit can make the right Bible verse work for you.

6. Pray according to the guide in Psalm 100. Record your experience.

7. As you encounter "God" connections, record these in your notebook. These experiences will strengthen your faith and confidence.

www.ingramcontent.com/pod-product-compliance
Lightning Source LLC
Chambersburg PA
CBHW071917070526
44583CB00016B/2030